how to be a
modern leader

how to
be a

MODERN

LEADER

By LAWRENCE K. FRANK

Association Press, New York

55

Printed in the United States of America
American Book–Stratford Press, Inc., New York

table of contents

1

kinds of leadership

How do you see yourself as a leader? What do you think are the duties and responsibilities of a leader? How do you see the leader operating, and what is most important for modern leadership?

Such questions have undoubtedly run through your mind. If you haven't started work with your group yet, you may have rehearsed what you expect to do, how you will start, and have imagined what your group will do and say. As a new or old hand at group leadership, you have been guided by some idea of what a leader is and does. This idea may or may not be desirable or appropriate. You may be thinking of leadership in terms that are no longer valid or appropriate today.

Before you commit yourself to any one kind of leadership, let us try to discover what is involved in being a leader today and see where we can get some further understanding of the leadership process. To do this, we should recognize that there are many different kinds of leadership, but that there is something common to all leadership. Also, we should understand the new meaning of organization and the *dynamics* of the leadership process.

After you have thoughtfully considered some of these issues and clarified your ideas, we can then look at some of the more concrete practical issues you face as a leader. Your approach to such questions as controversy, discipline and order, revising plans and programs, can be guided by these preliminary explorations into the leadership process.

Some, according to an old saying, are born to leadership, some achieve leadership, and others have leadership thrust upon them. Those who have leadership, so to speak, thrust upon them, are often perplexed, even baffled, by the responsibility which they must accept and try to utilize constructively. Some of this perplexity about what to do and how to act as a leader arises from the conflicting ideas about leaders. We have many beliefs and practices surviving from earlier days regarding leaders and leadership. These traditional ideas are becoming increasingly unsuitable, even destructive, in a democratic society. But we are not clear how to replace them. Today we are trying to develop a new conception of leadership and to learn how to be modern leaders.

A leader never functions in a vacuum; he must communicate in some way with his group, and the group must respond to him. So one important aspect of leadership is the organization or group setting in which a leader operates. Here we find a truly amazing range of human organizations in which leaders, from the top to the lowest ranks, operate according to an established code of conduct and prescribed relationships required by and for that organization.

Thus we see in a military organization a well-defined chain of command running from the commander-in-chief down through all the grades and ranks of officers and noncommissioned officers. Each exercises leadership functions as directed by the authority above, with penalties for any unauthorized actions or neglect of duty. This more or less authoritative leadership is probably the most familiar and most ancient pattern. It has been taken over and adapted to many other human organizations, such as most factories and even to some degree in education and organized athletics. In the military-type organization everyone knows his place and his specific duties and responsibilities. Everyone has to be obedient to those above and has authority over all those below him. Each is taught the necessity of maintaining that organizational pattern and procedure as strictly as possible under all circumstances. Leadership here, except perhaps for a few at the top, is limited, almost stereotyped, to what can and must be done, according to orders and regulations. A military leader is a *commander* who relies upon obedience.

At the other extreme, we see the spontaneous, unrehearsed leader who emerges in a crisis—some dire emergency, like a fire, a wreck, or an accident. He literally leads others, who may be paralyzed by fear, to safety, being quick to see possibilities of escape and courageous enough to start them moving in that direction. Here the leader has a function, but he operates without any assigned authority or defined responsibility; he is accepted by those who are desperately in need of guidance because he can lead them. After the crisis he may disappear and become anonymous again.

Something similar may happen when one person in a group suddenly expresses in words and actions an impulse to act violently. The group, acting as a mob, responds to this example by releasing their emotions, sometimes ignoring law and order, destroying property and killing people. They move ahead, believing they have a leader, but he may be as blind and confused as the group, not realizing what he is doing and why he is acting in this way. This kind of leadership has no authority or power to command as in a military unit, but operates through the spontaneous response of the group to someone who acts and directs their energies and channels their reactions.

There are other kinds of so-called leaders, like Hitler, who, by their eloquence and their skillful appeal to people's anxieties, can sway large groups of people. Those who are anxious and uncertain may gladly give up their freedom and offer their loyalty and devotion to such a person. They welcome opportunities to sacrifice themselves, feeling exalted in being used by their leader for whatever purposes he may choose. Then, too, there are leaders who are "born" to the position, like hereditary monarchs who are often only symbols surviving from the dim past when their ancestors were fighting leaders. Then there is a leadership which is a decorative function, often a "front" for those who actually decide and run the government.

Also there are leaders like Jesus, Buddha and, more recently, Gandhi, who claim no authority, exercise no power, but evoke allegiance of people by their unique personalities and the way of life they preach.

Each kind of leader, therefore, operates in a special kind of situation, a more or less organized group or purposeful setting, oriented to some specific goals or tasks. His leadership will be shaped, often strictly controlled, by the formal requirements, the purpose and directives of that organization. He must conform more or less to the pattern of the organization, military, industrial, and so on. But, being an individual personality, he has his own individualized ways of thinking, feeling, acting, and relating himself to others. Thus each leader will be different, exhibiting his own imagination, skills, courage, his capacity for understanding and for empathy (the ability to feel with others).

How to be a leader, a modern leader, who is aware of what he is doing in his leadership and is capable of evaluating and improving his own procedures and relationships, is a crucial task today. Often, without realizing, we utilize ideas and patterns from an earlier age, like the military pattern, which we still need and must use when required, although the old military style is changing. We must develop the kinds of leadership in all our group activities and classes that are appropriate to a free society and to the goals we are seeking in our organization. As will be noted later, boys and girls and young adolescents need the kind of leadership that will help them to grow up and mature. They need this kind of leadership especially when they come from homes where the parents are unwilling to let their child grow up and become increasingly independent for adult living.

There is no simple formula, no course of "ten easy lessons," despite the claims we often hear. In all human relations, there are no substitutes for sincerity, generosity, and genuine respect for others. Being a leader is a test both of our personal integrity and of our capacity to mature as a personality who increasingly learns to translate his goal values, his ethical aspirations, into his relations with others. As we shall see, the good leader in the modern sense is the one who is least inclined to act as the "boss," to pose as an expert who knows all the answers, to act as the dominating person in the group. He does not rely upon his position or prestige or authority, but upon his ability to exercise dynamic leadership by relating himself to his group and his group to him. The modern leader shares leadership with members of his group, encouraging and, if necessary, calling upon them to take the lead at different times.

2

what is common to all leaders

Let us consider leadership in both the formal and the informal, or the less-structured, organizations or situations, where people, young and old, seek or accept leadership as they participate in various kinds of group activities. These activities include games, physical exercise and athletic performances; folk dancing, dramatics (rehearsed or spontaneous); esthetic, artistic performances of music; choral singing and painting; classes, study and discussion groups; committees, neighborhood and community organizations. These may occur in factories, in stores, in offices, in camps, in schools and colleges, in churches, and in voluntary community organizations. Thus we shall be concerned with leaders of all kinds of groups—counselors of boys' and girls' clubs, scout masters, directors of choral and orchestra groups, adult education teachers, camp counselors, directors of physical education, dramatics, and recreational groups, young people's class and club advisers.

What we are discovering here applies to all leaders, including supervisors, executives in business, industry, and educational organizations, chairmen of committees, and the like. What the leader does and how he acts toward the group will vary, of course, with the size of the group or the meeting, but the leadership process will be largely the same.

Each organization may call for special knowledge and skills, for a specific content and methods or techniques. Nevertheless, all leaders are confronted with the same basic situation: they must function as leaders and utilize the processes of leadership, whatever specific purposes they may seek or whatever specialized activities they may be conducting.

In the same way, every teacher, whatever the subject he teaches, must use language and gestures, employ symbols, and establish some relations with the members of his class as a teacher. The teacher has to foster learning, the mastery of subject matter and skills, whatever he or she teaches. So the leader of any group has to exercise leadership functions and utilize the leadership-follower processes whether he leads a club, a discussion group, a cabin unit at camp, a team, or a committee. Thus, in whatever kind of group, young or old—recreational, educational, or otherwise—the leader faces similar tasks and needs the same basic orientation and understanding of his role and of the potentialities of the group he is leading.

The older or adult leader of adolescents or young boys and girls should recognize that he has a different status as an older, more experienced person. His group expects him to be more aware of situations and to be more responsible. At the same time its members want the older leader to treat them as individuals who have some dignity and whose aspirations he will respect. Most adults, as parents and teachers, have for too long been more or less authoritative, giving orders, demanding obedience, with little or no discussion or even explanation to children. The adult leader of a group of younger persons often tends to follow this same parental pattern. His group may, at least outwardly, accept him in that role. But he will fail to be a leader in the sense we are here discussing, because he does not recognize their desire to grow up and mature. He does not give them a feeling of being capable of self-discipline. He does not evoke the group's latent strengths nor create situations in which the dynamics of the group can operate.

Such authoritative leaders often block or retard the maturation of their group members. Children, and especially adolescents, need all possible help in learning to be increasingly autonomous, to do things as steps toward self-accepted goals, to achieve worthwhile tasks, to be self-governing. They cannot develop these capacities all at once; they may fumble and alternate between more mature conduct and more or less silliness and even disorder. But slowly, with helpful guidance and encouragement by the leaders, they will be able to accept responsibility for self-direction and for sustained effort at achieving goals of their own choosing.

It often happens that the leader of a club or other group of young people, especially adolescents, does not realize how his attitude may perpetuate the immaturity, the dependency, and the helplessness of a boy or girl. Thus he may establish a close, almost affectionate, relationship with a boy or girl who welcomes this relationship. Such a leader may say, "That boy will do anything for me," without realizing that the boy's good conduct or efforts are primarily to win the approval of the leader. By this personal devotion to the leader, he evades the burden of being well-behaved or competent *on his own account*. In such cases the boy or girl may continue to be dependent upon adults at the time when the young person should be increasingly autonomous and willing to accept guidance and supervision—but not just to win adult acceptance. This does not mean that a leader should be aloof and impersonal. He should, however, be aware of how his relationship to an individual in the group may become a handicap to the development of that individual as a personality. He should realize that a leader who thinks of himself as a benevolent, loving big brother or sister, or father or mother to his group, may be using his group for his own personal emotional needs or self-glorification.

3

the meaning of organization

Whether he takes on an already organized group or has to create a new group, a leader should clearly understand what organization means. He may find that his group has had a previous leader who did not understand the organization process. In such cases, he must organize his group as if it were a new group except that its members will be better acquainted with each other. If he has to create a new group, made up of individuals who do not know each other, he must help them to organize.

Organizations have long been considered as more or less fixed, often rigid, forms or arrangements. When we ask what is the organization, we point to an organizational chart or diagram showing the various positions, departments or divisions, the lines of authority and command as the organization. These are only pictures or diagrams, however, which do not tell us what an organization does or how it operates.

We are learning to think of a human organization, a military unit, a factory, a social group, or a committee as a pattern or configuration which is continually changing but which nevertheless persists. For example, the eleven men who make up a football team create the team as an organization by the way each member of the team plays his specialized position in that team—guard, halfback, end, and so on. Each player acts always in relation to the other members of the team. He is continually alert to what the others are doing and continually responding to one or more members of the team. The organization may be viewed as this dynamic, ever-changing activity, within a flexible pattern, which the members of the team constantly maintain. The team in action on the field is engaged in a series of these rapid shifts and alterations in formations for each play, but each member helps to maintain the team organization by always acting in relation to the others. The individual who "plays" to the grandstand for personal glory is not a good teammate. He may lose the game and ruin the team organization by his failure to play with the others.

Organization is a circular process, a dynamic operation which, we are beginning to recognize, occurs in whatever is organized. It involves doing something to and with others so that what they do in response will provide for the next activity, again calling for individual action that is continually oriented and related to the others. It is as if each member of the organization or team were stimulating, provoking, seeking from the others the responses which would enable him to take his next action, to which they will respond by giving him a further occasion to act. It is like the actors in a play who know their lines and, at their cues, act and speak to give the other actors their cues, and so on, as the play continues.

Organization and team play or teamwork cannot occur unless each member of the group has some understanding of what the group is organized to do and how he can function in the group in this reciprocal fashion. Indeed, we might say that what makes the individuals into members of the organization is this shared idea, belief, expectation, and aspiration which each translates into his performance, contributing his individualized participation to the group performance so that it becomes organized and related, and can function productively.

Let us think of an orchestra, made up of sometimes a hundred or more musicians: each has learned to play his specific instrument—violin, cello, bass viol, trombone, trumpet, flute, oboe, bassoon, drum, cymbals, and so on. By practicing alone and then rehearsing together, they learn to synchronize, to blend, to play together. Each musician must play his specific notes at the right time and in the precise sequence on his instrument; these individual sounds may, by themselves, be irregular, discordant, unrelated or monotonous, but when blended with the other sounds at the appropriate time, it all becomes music, sometimes of overwhelming intensity and beauty. This is what happens, too, in a choral group with part singers.

Here again we see organization as a flexible pattern, a persistent but ever-changing configuration, an active, dynamic *togetherness*. This does not destroy or diminish the individuality of those who make up the whole, but rather it enables them to attain, by their concerted, reciprocal activities, what no one alone could achieve. Each musician, each singer, has a clear understanding of both the total composition and of his individual participation in that whole. He has a belief in his essential, indispensable role and at the same time an expectation that others will recognize and will respond in their individualized way to his performance, thereby helping him to contribute more effectively and meaningfully to the whole. He can respect himself and find fulfillment of his aspirations to be a good musician, a fine singer, as he participates in this organized group performance because the group calls forth his best efforts and at the same time enables him to evoke similar strivings from the others in the group. We cannot too strongly emphasize this reciprocal relationship, not just of one person to another (which, as in friendship, in marriage, in parent-child relations, has its own dynamics and fulfillments). In the musical group it is a relationship of one to many and also of that many to each one, without loss of each one's identity, individuality, and self-respect, as in many other kinds of organizations.

But here we come to the crux of this kind of organization—namely, the leader or conductor of the orchestra or chorus. Ideally he serves as the personification of each musician's hopes and faith in the objectives of the orchestra and of the performer's desire to be orchestrated with the others. Only as each believes in the conductor and recognizes that his direction is essential to the group performance does he fully enter into and actively participate in the performance. Sustained by a belief in the conductor's musicianship and by his own aspirations to give a good performance, the orchestra member will accept criticisms, even sharp rebukes and strong directives, because he recognizes that these are all aimed at improvement of what he and his fellow players are seeking—an ever better performance as a whole. In some concerts a musician may sit for several hours doing nothing until there arrives the moment when he must play a short passage, perhaps only one or two notes, which no one in the audience may hear as such, but he knows that his brief contribution is essential to the whole. He is sustained by his belief in the ideal of a nearly perfect performance of that musical composition and by his confidence in himself to make his contribution—a confidence that derives from the conductor's beliefs in his capacity and calm expectation that at the precise moment he will perform and meet that expectation.

The orchestra is a good illustration of what we are trying to understand as organization, but not the only one. Teamwork, team play, a well-balanced theatrical group, the intent, sharply focused team of surgeons, nurses, and anesthetists collaborating in the operating room—these are similar organizational configurations where individuals give their utmost to the group endeavor. They are aided, guided, directed, synchronized, enabled to use their energies, their skills, by their self-confidence and reliance upon each other. But these efforts are evoked and sustained by someone who acts as their leader, whatever name, title, or position he may carry. Sometimes one musician will play a solo part alone, or with the others accompanying him or blending or contrasting with his playing as he takes the lead. Likewise in a club or committee, we find individuals of different backgrounds, skills, and experience, which each can contribute, who take the "lead" so to speak, in clarifying, planning, suggesting decisions, and in turn evoke the contribution of others. This is what is meant by sharing in the leadership process.

We should think a bit about that word *evoke* as contrasted with more familiar words, such as order, command, direct, cause, stimulate and similar terms which emphasize someone in authority or power who issues orders, gives commands, stimulates or, to use a more recent word, "motivates." All of these imply a different kind of organization and a different relationship to the leader. This is what usually occurs in a more rigid, coercive kind of organized group where performance is primarily governed by rewards and penalties, often by fear and by submissive obedience, a reluctant, often halfhearted compliance. The leader in such situations is rarely a conductor, the elected captain of a team, the "first" among equals, as the old Latin phrase put it—*primus inter pares*. Such a "leader" may drive, coerce, put on pressure, threaten punishment, or promise rewards, relying upon the organizational framework, his authority, his power, his right to "fire" or expel or withhold rewards as a way of keeping individuals in line. In contrast, the leadership we are discussing here is concerned with integrating individuals so that they feel they are primarily members of the group and have loyalty to their group as well as to their leader. The morale of the group is sustained by the leader's skill in maintaining their group feeling of belonging and working together. This contrasts with the practice of relying upon individual obedience or devotion to the leader as their major interest or concern.

When speaking of *evoking* from people their full, active group participation, we are not primarily concerned with an impersonal organization. Rather, we are focusing on persons, live individuals: each a personality, with hopes and expectations, aspirations, and feelings which the leader *evokes* in order to channel or direct them to the performance of what they are ready or even eager to achieve. He may evoke better performance from one person by candid criticism which makes that person recognize his failure to live up to his own aspirations and shows him where and how he should improve. As such, criticism will be accepted as helpful and constructive. The person thus criticized will try harder and more carefully to attain the improved performance, whether it be musical or athletic, dancing, or acting, or learning, or treating a patient. This kind of evocation ordinarily occurs, however, only in some kind of organizational group setting.

This description of teamwork, as orchestrating diverse persons and skills upon a common theme, offers a dynamic conception of what we mean by organization. It helps us to see the setting, situation, configuration, and context in which leadership occurs. It is to be contrasted with the familiar ideas of organization as a coercive, authoritarian, leader-dominated operation, within a more or less rigid framework of rules, regulations, and penalties, and with submissive obedience to commands. Organization can be, and frequently is, just this kind of configuration within which people work, serve, perform tasks, lending themselves to the extent that they find it necessary to do as they are told. The "leader" in such a setting ordinarily does little beyond transmitting orders, supervising and following up his group in carrying out these orders so that he, as leader, can satisfy his superior's orders or directives. Sometimes, those who are asked to be leaders or who undertake the role of a leader know only this kind of organization. They exhibit this kind of leadership although they are called upon to function in a different setting and with people who are not under the same restraints and compulsions as in these more rigid organizations.

Teams or "orchestras," and similarly organized groups, operate through shared goals and the aspirations of each member of the group. Therefore, such organizations require clearly stated and well-understood purposes or aims that each member of the group has accepted, not because they are imposed, but as aims, goals, ideals which others will join in working for, but each in his own way. Increasingly, he finds under good leadership that *his* way and their ways blend or fuse so that the individual and the group can act and think in concert. This is more than being told by the leader what is expected and how to do it. It takes time and respect for others' ideas, willingness to listen to others as they listen to him, for any idea or goal to become clearly understood and accepted by each as *his* goal. He has to have time and reassurance from the leader and from other members of the group as he interprets or translates this common idea, this group objective into his own individualized way of thinking and feeling. Obviously, an individual will rarely give up his own personal ideas or abandon his own purposes completely. But to the extent that he, as an individual personality, finds it possible to attain his purposes within the group program, he will be able to participate freely and actively, especially if the group and the leader will recognize and accept his individual feelings and strivings. In such a case, the leader has to help the group to understand the individual member, as we shall see later.

The less the members of a group are subject to the

pressures and coercions often found in military, industrial, and other strongly purposive organizations and objectives, the more significant are their personal individual aims and patterns, and consequently the more dynamic the organization can be. If an individual is not compelled to participate, not dominated by authority or by fear of penalties or expulsion, he can maintain his own individualized ways of thinking, acting, and feeling. The leader's role is to foster this process, encouraging each one to be himself but, at the same time, to share the group thinking and planning.

Too often we stubbornly cling to an idea, insist upon our way of doing things, and try to block or defeat others because we do not know how to escape from our self-defeating patterns without feeling humiliated or defeated as inferior. Or we don't know how to attain our personal goals except by attacking or resisting others. We cannot belong to a group until we are able to reorganize our ideas, relearn how to act, to relate ourselves, and so to participate with others while still retaining our own individuality, our personal identity. This is possible in a flexible dynamic organization when we understand more clearly what organization involves as a functioning process, the articulation of individualized strivings toward the common aims of the group members. But we need encouragement and reassurance in order to give up or reduce our self-assertiveness and learn how to work with others.

Here again we see how this dynamic conception of organization helps us to realize that the organizing of a group takes place by this process of entering into and assimilating the group's underlying purpose, aims, and modes of operation. This is what we mean when we speak of "group dynamics," as we shall see in Chapter 4—that is, evoking voluntary, individual growth and action which comes from the interpersonal, reciprocal relations of group members as controlled or guided by the purposes and objectives of the group.

Only when each member of the group has gone through this process in his own way and at his own rate of assimilation does an organization come into being. Think of a team which must have prolonged "skull practice" as well as drill and coaching and active practice in order to become a team and to achieve *organization,* as a functioning process involving all members of the group but in their individualized patterns of participation. And rarely is an organization composed of those who are equally alert, responsive, skillful, capable of taking any one of the various positions or posts. Indeed, organization, like an animal organism, becomes possible only by more or less specialization, differentiation, division of labor, like the heart, lungs, stomach, arms and legs, nervous system, and sensory apparatus. Human organizations, however, are not inherited, built-in patterns; they have to be learned and developed. Those who make up an organization must learn how to think and act together in order to participate in an organization. The organization need not be elaborate or highly skilled like a team or orchestra. If, however, it is to have any vitality, any capacity for continued operation and increasing effectiveness for whatever it is trying to do, this sharing of ideas, of assumptions and expectations, is essential. In a military-type organization, the members today are given a preliminary indoctrination, an initial orientation to what they are supposed to know and believe, and how they are supposed to act. Often, however, this is just "telling 'em," with little opportunity to question, to express doubts, and to seek further clarification.

This process of *organizing* the group, creating the shared framework of ideas and purposes and reciprocal relationships, not only gives the group its basic patterns of operation, but also establishes the kind of leadership relation in which that group will function and in which its leader must carry on his role. All this takes time—a seemingly endless process sometimes—as, one after another, members of the group ask questions, object, offer divergent or rival views, argue and debate, become emotionally aroused or sullen and withdrawn. It tries the patience of the leader and strains the loyalty of the group members who may secretly or openly wish someone to terminate the endless talking so that they can "get going." But if the leader acts too soon, tries to resolve the situation by invoking an agreement for which they are not ready, the group organization may take place but without the commitment that alone makes a coherent and dynamic organization.

Often one or more members are still unclear, unconvinced, unable to see in their own terms what the group is seeking, what the group assumes and expects as a sort of basic frame of reference. These members may then persistently impede and even, without intention, sabotage the group—they are not yet "organized" within the group, not yet persuaded or convinced, and so they are unable to respond to the group and the leader as active participating

27

group members. Often such individuals are still fighting or resisting someone elsewhere—father, big brother, or teacher. They "let out" their hostility upon the leader or the group without realizing what they are doing. It may take a long time for such individuals to feel comfortable in the group, to recognize that they do not need to fight or be on guard, in order to be accepted.

It has been customary, when setting up an organization, to draw up a charter or constitution with by-laws as a formal statement which all members are expected to accept and abide by. These statements, designating the powers, authority, the rules and procedures, supplemented by parliamentary rules of order, often serve to create and maintain an organization. But these formal declarations and rules must be interpreted and applied to become effective. Today our society is made up increasingly of people with often different traditional beliefs, expectations, and assumptions, even different codes of conduct and different ideas of what is considered fair, just, and right. Accordingly, we cannot rely as formerly upon these formal constitutions and rules for operating an organization. These seemingly clear and plain words may have different meanings for people who interpret them in the light of their different traditional beliefs and patterns.

If we grasp this dynamic conception of organization, recognize that it involves reciprocal relations or responses in the group which become the familiar, customary patterns when once the group has been "organized" and so is ready to function, then we can begin to understand more clearly what leadership involves. Obviously, the leader must actively lead in this initial process of organization since his leadership is essential to start the process. Occasionally, a leader enters into an already organized and operating group which may or may not need to be redirected to more effective functioning; but sooner or later every group exhibits its own peculiar way of operating in which the kind and quality of its leadership appears sometimes clearly visible, sometimes less apparent, but still of major significance.

4

dynamics of the leadership process

As a leader facing a group, you want and need to understand what is going on in the group—not just what the members may be saying or doing, but what they are thinking, feeling, wondering about, and expecting of you. This means understanding the dynamics of a group and recognizing the processes operating in the group.

When a number of persons come together to talk, to play, or to work together *as a group*, they start a process which we are just beginning to understand. Each member of the group continues to be an individual personality with his own personal, private beliefs, expectations, aspirations—all his characteristic ways of thinking and of feeling. But when he enters into a group and begins to relate himself to the other members, he begins to experience a different orientation, a new way of feeling and of acting for which we have no adequate words.

For example, a group of boys come together and decide to play ball or some group game. Almost immediately each one begins to act as a member of the group or team so that whatever he does is now directed to the group-team and how they respond to him. It is as if for a while he puts aside or ignores his own personal, individualized ideas and desires in order to belong, to think and act, to feel with the other members of the group-team. Something in each one is evoked so that what he does is now primarily directed to the others who in turn look to and respond to him. Instead of a collection of separate individuals, each pursuing his own objectives and only partially concerned about the others, there is now a group that has become more or less organized. As we realized in our discussion of organization earlier, this means that each member of the group is related to the others and they are related to him in a circular process, a continually changing but persistent relationship guided by the leader. Whatever anyone says or does evokes a response from the others, and he must then recognize their response in whatever he does next. Since each one of the group is involved in this circular process, a very dynamic operation goes on.

It is now a self-energizing group, evoking the capacities of the members in different degrees, through this circular process we have been discussing. By acting together, evoking from each other and responding to each other, a dynamic process operates, arising from this concerted reciprocal relationship.

When the members of a group have developed this we-feeling, their energies are released so that they can be more productive, creative, and responsive than in their ordinary activities and relations. At the same time, they are organized by being oriented and directed, and they become more purposeful as they accept their group aims and purposes. This means that they ignore or minimize what is at that time not relevant nor appropriate to the group activity (such as personal jealousy, playing to the gallery, or trying to "scare off" someone). They find a kind of self-discipline, through accepting a self-chosen task to which each can loyally and effectively give himself. The emergence of the group as an organized whole (from a number of separate, unrelated individuals) with their altered performance (individually and collectively), gives rise to the dynamics of the group. Their energies may be directed into a variety of channels and utilized for various objectives of which "group dynamics" (see a definition of this on page 26) and "group decisions" are familiar examples.

Creative expressions of the dynamics of the group are revealed in group discussions of a play, movie, story or novel, or when members of a group act spontaneously, perhaps at camp, some dramatic incident, give a hand puppet show, enter into a "group conversation" about their traditions and festivals. In these it often happens that members of the group find themselves thinking, speaking, reacting emotionally in ways they never realized they were capable of doing before. They gain insights, see meanings, develop sympathy, and often have an experience that initiates a new stage in their maturation as they participate and respond to the dynamics of the group. Their feeling of belonging, of sharing, of finding approval in the group gives the necessary provocation and also the reassurance which individuals need to revise their ideas and to alter their customary patterns of action, thinking, and relationships. These group experiences often start processes in the individual that continue to operate after the group meeting; he mulls over them later on, rehearses them, talks about them with others, as he revises or reconstructs his customary beliefs and expectations. In a very real sense, he discovers himself, as having potentialities for development, capacities for maturing which were latent or dormant, waiting to be evoked by congenial company when his usual defenses and resistances were not active or necessary.

Today we are faced with many new situations and are expected to understand and be guided by the many new ideas and assumptions which are operating in almost every field of human living. We all need these group experiences to help us change our customary ideas and to learn new ways of thinking and acting. The leader today, therefore, has this responsibility of being a "change agent," one who facilitates these revisions in people's ideas and relations. Yet, to do this, he must recognize that individuals need time to reorganize their thinking and to work out their own acceptance of altered patterns.

Now it should be remembered that what we call group dynamics is not a new invention. This name has been applied to a process that has been operating for ages in human affairs but only recently has it been recognized and studied. We are now intentionally utilizing it in group therapy, and increasingly in group organizations such as industry, business, education, recreation, and even in some military units. What has been practiced intuitively, as we say, by those who without conscious awareness or deliberate reasoning have guided, directed, commanded units, is being recognized now as central in the leadership process. Here the designated leader serves as the catalyst, the enzyme, the instigator of this dynamic process in group formation and operation. As this is more clearly understood, the role of the leader changes from that of boss, commander, expert, chairman, authority, and similar terms for superior, powerful persons with authority and sanction. He functions as *a member of the group,* but with a special responsibility as leader to evoke leadership from different members of his group. He must relate himself to everyone in the group but at the same time foster and maintain the relation of each to all other members in the group, as well as to himself.

Though the leader is the more active agent in the leadership process, the group he leads is essential to and shares in the leadership process. Only as the leader evokes these responses can he function as a leader and help the members to attain what they seek. The leader is dependent upon his group for his own encouragement and development as a leader. His confidence in himself as leader grows as the group responds to him, and this response to him evokes and strengthens his capacity as leader. We see then that leadership is essentially a process of circular, interpersonal relations—of leader to group, of members of the group to each other, and all to the leader. Each one speaks, acts, and feels together because each one belongs to the group and may exert leadership in the group with the support and encouragement of the designated leader.

Usually the leader finds that in his group there is one person who is "best liked" by the others: he may not have the "best ideas" or even good judgment, but he is liked and has popularity. Such a "best liked" person can be of great help to the designated or task leader because he can keep the group in good temper, help to relieve tension, and maintain group morale. The leader should recognize such a person as his most valuable assistant and rely upon him for this kind of collaboration. Above all, the leader must not compete with such a "best liked" person for the group's admiration or feel jealous of his popularity.

Though every group and leader will be different, with different purposes, needs and auspices, the operations and relations in all groups which are involved in the leadership process are nevertheless quite similar. We shall now discuss them as further steps in understanding leadership.

1110033

5

the group purpose and objectives

In any group activity, whether it is a recreational group engaged in folk dancing, or a team of workers, athletes, soldiers, an educational or a discussion group, or a committee, there is some purpose or aim, some task or goal to be attained. One of the major difficulties in the organization of a group and in its effective operation is in developing a shared understanding, an acceptance, and a genuine commitment to that group objective. If we remember that a group is composed of individual persons, each a personality with his own individualized beliefs and assumptions, his peculiar expectations, ways of acting and responding, of feeling and not-feeling, we shall realize that these separate individuals are living in quite different "private worlds." They may all be together in one place, exposed to the same public situations and people, listening to the same statements, looking at each other, and responding to the leader. But each one will be seeing a different situation, perceiving different people, hearing different words or at least giving them different meanings, and continually responding with feelings of acceptance, admiration, or rejection. Moreover, each one may come to the group with the hope and expectation of finding what each might describe in the same words, but each will have his own individualized version of that purpose or expectation, his own belief, sometimes intense conviction about the way to organize, operate, proceed toward that goal, as he conceives or expects it. Sometimes a person will believe he is right and everyone else is wrong, or he may lack any personal convictions and eagerly seek someone to tell him what to think and do. There are many, many variations of these personal attitudes and activities, since each member of the group is more or less a unique personality.

There is a wide variety of individual personalities in every group—each with his own ideas and feelings—which we recognize and often find very difficult to deal with. Nevertheless, these differences are only variations around the general patterns of our culture. A visitor from another land would see these differences as of little significance compared with the underlying similarity of patterns we all share. It takes great originality and genuinely creative capacities to be truly different, to have original ideas and conceptions, such as are developed from time to time by the artist, poet, scientist, or mystic.

We can understand the great importance of these individualized beliefs and actions if we will remember that each one of us is striving to be a person, to be and to act as an individual in accordance with our traditions. For thousands of years the Judaic-Christian tradition has emphasized the worth of the individual personality as unique and precious. We grow up believing we must somehow be an individual and maintain our individuality, defending it when it is attacked or slighted. Sometimes we aggressively seek recognition and prestige as a symbolic expression of our individual self.

Now most of us are not geniuses, with original, creative powers; we are normal, usual persons with varying degrees of intelligence, skills, energies, and sometimes special aptitudes. So of necessity we must use the common stock of ideas and beliefs, the accepted and normal patterns as ways of dealing with the world and other people. But in order to act and feel as individuals, we may emphasize our own personal, special versions of these common beliefs, these accepted convictions and practices. At the same time, we want to be like everyone else because we have no resources other than the accepted ways of living and thinking. We often feel uneasy and even anxious when we find ourselves "out of step" with others; but while we are trying to be like others and to be accepted by them as normal, we are also striving to be different. Each of us, for example, will wear clothes like others we associate with, some of us being more or less quickly responsive to changing fashions. But each wears those more or less similar clothes "with a difference," varying details to accent and express our individual tastes and personal style.

These differences in beliefs, in patterns of speech, of action, and of ways of relating oneself to situations and people just because they are basically so similar may become sensitive spots, "sanctuaries," which each of us strives to maintain and to defend against others as expression of our individualized personality. We may not be so opposed and resistant to what someone says as we appear to be when we express an opinion or make a judgment that contradicts that person. We may take a strong negative or opposed position rejecting what has been said, primarily as a way of maintaining our individuality, and asserting our own position to call attention to ourself. Indeed, we often proclaim a contrary viewpoint only to find we are "out on a limb" and cannot give any reasonable grounds for our opposition. Or we may insist that the reasons offered in support of what someone has urged are all wrong and that our reasons are good and must be accepted first before we will concur in what is often clearly the most sound and appropriate judgment.

These individualized responses are highly diversified. They are often expressive of many different beliefs and feelings, of what may be utterly irrelevant in that situation. Yet this may be very important to the individual who expresses his views and often challenges anyone to differ from him. In so far as his statements arise from his purely private affairs, often from his relationship elsewhere (such as his family), they may be continuations of disputes and of conflicts which began years ago in childhood. They may even be the verbalization of arguments he has been carrying on with himself as he speaks aloud what he has been saying to himself in that inner speech we carry on in our private worlds. Sometimes the leader or another member of the group touches off something in an individual who thereupon reacts strongly although no one has given him any provocation or said anything that was directed to him.

These and many other aspects of the individuality of persons may be exhibited in a group as each one feels threatened, worried about himself, anxiously looking for an opportunity to assert his personal views and purposes and to oppose or combat others. At this point there is no group, only a collection of individuals, each preoccupied with his own individuality, even when he may be present in the group to discuss, plan, and act as a group. Somehow these highly individualized personalities, each more or less wrapped up in his concerns, need to be helped to organize a group and develop the dynamics of the group. Here is where the leadership process must operate if the individual members are to become a group and to function effectively. One of the initial steps is to evolve some kind of group purpose or objective so that these individualized persons can and will be able to share and "organize" themselves into a functioning group oriented to some common goals.

One way of doing this is often used in organizations where the individual, as an individual, is put through a series of experiences in which what he thinks, feels, desires, and expects is not very important and must be ignored and forgotten. He is made to realize that he is one in a group, a well-drilled machine, of importance and value only as he is quickly responsive to the orders or commands he must obey. This sometimes is sought in highly trained athletic teams under the hand of a coach who trains each player to do as he is told if he wants to be on that team. School classrooms are sometimes run in a similar manner by a teacher who aims, not at a group, but at a well-trained class of obedient pupils, each responsive to the teacher's orders. These and similar examples illustrate the long-accepted type of authoritarian leader who uses the members of a group as instruments for whatever purposes he, or someone above him, has set as the objective.

If, however, the group and their leader are not to function in this way that ignores and suppresses the individuality, some other ways of functioning are needed. It has long been recognized that some kind of planned activity offers an often acceptable beginning for group formation. Thus a group may initially decide to take a trip, undertake a simple project, play a game, talk over their recent experiences. The action may be one already selected, as when individuals seek to join a team or recreational group established for a designated purpose. Or it may be a more general objective, an action to be decided upon by the group, after discussion of both ends and means. Sometimes the longer-term purpose is not declared or recognized in the beginning so that an initial, short-term goal or job serves to bring the group together. This then provides an opportunity to explore the group process where it is not likely to provoke undue conflict or dissension. In this initial stage a certain amount of vagueness or uncertainty may be advantageous since it gives the members of the group-to-be-formed some reassurance that they are not committed and are not bound by the group.

But sooner or later some kind of declared aim or purpose becomes essential since only as the members of the group accept this joint aim can they begin to relate themselves as persons to these common goals. They can then enter into group formation and begin to operate in ways that produce an organization, as we described this in Chapter 3, only by developing a *common* set of goals. Some jointly shared idea or objective, to be effective, must supersede and replace the highly individualized beliefs and aims of each member so that he will recognize others as engaged in the same pursuit, giving to and receiving from others what makes each a group member. If the purpose is some specific action they can all undertake, then each can retain his individual beliefs and reasons for joining in a concerted endeavor. He can "go along" with the others without having to accept their different opinions or surrendering his own beliefs and reasons, so long as they can agree on what to do and how it is to be done. This seeming unanimity is fostered by the way each agrees to the formulation of their purpose, interpreting it according to his own ideas and meaning of words which may be quite at variance with others. This is frequently the case when a group of people has reached such a verbal agreement by deliberately avoiding too much discussion and letting each one make such mental reservations as he wishes so long as he will vote for the proposal. Sometimes this serves to hold a group together while they get better acquainted, learn to trust each other and the leader, and so begin to operate as a group.

In any kind of personal relations, especially of more than two persons, some assumptions must be made, something must be taken for granted as the only basis of communication. Thus, for example, language is accepted with the usual common meanings and interpretations. People will ordinarily refrain from hair-splitting definitions and prolonged arguments over words and phrases, if they are genuinely eager to find some common basis for discussion and decision. But today groups are made up of people from a variety of traditional backgrounds and also of people who are becoming increasingly critical of many of our usual assumptions and expectations. To formulate some common purposes, to develop some consensus among members of a group with different traditions and differing degrees of critical awareness has become difficult.

Even when people come together in a meeting which is organized and operated according to accepted parliamentary rules, difficulties arise since we are no longer a homogeneous people with common standards and goals. Thus someone may move and be seconded and then debate a proposed resolution, according to parliamentary rules of order, and yet the group does not arrive at a consensus. Majority rule, which operated effectively among people of common backgrounds as a fair way of deciding among alternative actions, all governed by similar beliefs and convictions, may become a way of coercing people, of "putting things over" in a struggle for power or for mutual self-defeat. In such meetings, the rival leaders marshal their followers to debate and vote according to the tactical needs of contending factions or parties. Voting settles nothing except as it helps to shape the next contest for power. This procedure, while glaringly apparent in political affairs, is also found in professional associations, in social clubs, recreational affairs, even educational groups, where objectives, goals have become confused or forgotten in the struggles of rival leaders and factions.

Just because this is so frequent, it becomes increasingly important to establish and maintain groups in which there can be genuine and sincere efforts to arrive at common understanding, acceptable goals, and modes of group operation. This takes time, with often prolonged and repeated sessions which become meaningful when we realize that each member of the group must, in his own way and at his own rate of progress, achieve that common understanding and sharing of beliefs and of purposes. This alone makes it possible to participate in the group process.

Sometimes action groups, eager to reach group decisions and get started on a program, seemingly may reach a high degree of consensus but go forward with an undeclared load of conflicting beliefs and expectations which later emerge or explode into open conflict and disintegration of the group. This is the constant threat to any group of people who come together to pool their grievances and exert their combined pressures to get some change or improvement. They are held together by their shared resentment or anxiety, but they lack any other basis for group thinking and even for group action in any other area. At the other extreme, we find groups, such as some religious organizations, which uphold a common body of beliefs, principles, and standards, though individuals may diverge about the precise meaning and application of those shared beliefs.

These are all relevant to the understanding of the leadership process where, as pointed out, the leader is not imposing an authoritarian pattern but is engaged in helping a group to organize around an idea, a set of beliefs and assumptions which they can accept as a common core of their thinking and action. They continue as individualized persons but learn to relate themselves to each other, actively participating in the leadership process by contributing to the group thinking and planning and selecting of objectives. These objectives may be as varied as there are groups of people and sponsors for such groups, but the need for leadership will be similar in all these different groups.

6

leadership in action

The preceding discussions become operational when we see the leader, an individual person, undertaking the leadership role with a group. According to this approach, it is not so much a question of special skills, techniques, and specific procedures, of detailed job analysis, but of understanding the roles the leader must assume and how he can create and maintain this circular reciprocal process of shared leadership in and through these roles. Since we are becoming accustomed to "role playing" as a device useful in group situations, we should be clear that the leadership process is not "role playing" as often interpreted. The leader is not *playing* a role, like an actor who plays a part, wearing a costume and speaking according to the character he is impersonating—which often is a very useful productive procedure in certain situations. The leader accepts and takes on his roles as a genuine, sincere, and personal commitment to the group; and in those roles he establishes relations with individual members of the group and with the group as a functioning whole. He is not impersonating someone, pretending or "make-believing," as in role playing, where such performances may have a desirable purpose. Rather the leader should be as sincere, honest, genuine as he can be while he actively participates in the leadership process which he must establish through his relations with group members. This does not mean that it is sufficient for the leader to be just well-meaning. Like a physician, he must establish confidence in the group, a conviction that he can be trusted and relied upon and that he in turn will trust them and treat them with respect as personalities. This is indeed a heavy responsibility and a demanding task which tests the leader's integrity as a person. A "smooth operator," a backslapper, an outwardly friendly but inwardly hostile or demanding personality, may serve as a "leader" for a while but no amount of technique or surface charm will serve as a substitute for the kind of genuine personal relating to others which good leadership requires.

Obviously, the good leader with these desirable capacities has to develop, to learn, and to mature. The very demands of leadership are conducive to this kind of maturation where the leader becomes increasingly a productive personality capable of evoking from others what they would like to be, helping them to live up to their own aspirations. Here we see how the circular reciprocal process we talked of earlier becomes operational when the leader, by evoking the potentialities of others, thereby develops his own potentialities. His own sincerity and generosity provide the occasions for others to speak and act sincerely and generously. This is what might be called a "virtuous circle" as contrasted with the familiar vicious circle of mutual distrust and deterioration.

This productive, evocative role cannot be "played" as an artifice except perhaps by a thoroughly corrupted person who has learned to manipulate persons and to dissimulate before a group. The kind of leadership roles we are discussing are taken on as a commitment, not only to the group but to oneself, as a sort of dedication. This does not mean being solemn and formal about oneself nor pretending to be completely unselfish or disinterested. It does mean that the leader enters into his leadership as a personality with his individual aims and aspirations, but not as a power-seeking individual or a manipulator. Above all, he should have genuine respect for those he seeks to lead. A leader of a group may have a feeling of condescension to the members, with an image of himself as a superior, stooping down to help these "poor people," "unfortunate poor children," "helpless youth," and so on. He may try to conceal this attitude and to put on a "front," but his group sooner or later will discover it and show their resentment if not rejection.

Thus the leader's role involves a continuous endeavor to build up each individual member's self-confidence, to increase his self-respect and his personal dignity, because lack of these, as we are discovering, may be expressed in every kind of self-defeating and group-destroying behavior. But building up a person's self-respect is not a question of using some special technique of flattering or insincere praise. Each individual's image of himself reflects the treatment he receives from others, and the way a leader treats the individual as a personality whom he genuinely recognizes and respects, despite that person's sometimes disturbing and annoying behavior, is what genuinely communicates.

Today when we read and hear so much about methods and techniques for creating good impressions, gaining attention, winning friends by calculated procedures, we must be continually on guard against these insidious devices. Likewise, we must be aware of how easy it is to get publicity and prestige by sacrificing one's own integrity as a person. The leader entering upon his office, sometimes uncertain and apprehensive, may be attracted to these "get popular quickly" practices because of his feeling of weakness and inexperience. But these may only increase his weakness because they do not evoke his strengths, his capacity to relate himself as one person to another, each of whom likes and respects the other. In a friendship, two persons are not concerned primarily with each other's failings and weaknesses, but with each other's strengths and potentialities which they mutually evoke and so find their relationship a happy and productive reciprocity. In a way, the leader becomes the friend of every member of the group but does not stir up envy and jealousy by showing favoritism or partiality to any one of them. Indeed, the leader may find that some individuals are not to his liking, but he must not reject these persons nor neglect them.

Leadership calls, however, for more than interpersonal relations: there are also the dynamics of the group, the channels of communication which hold the group together like a magnetic field in which each particle of iron occupies a relation to all the other particles and every change in one is accompanied by alterations in all the others. This ever-changing dynamic configuration becomes focused or oriented by the group acceptance of its aims and purposes which give rise to the program or tasks the group will undertake to achieve under a good leader.

7

common problems of leadership

The first problem of a leader is to know his group which means not merely learning their names, but discovering what kinds of personalities they are and what roles in the group each one takes. As Fritz Redl pointed out some years ago:

In most groups the one or other youngster begins to assume a certain "role" in his relation to the rest of the group. This means that this youngster will—partly independent of his personality and special needs or interests in other respects —tend to assume the same attitude under certain conditions with a high degree of predictability. The following are examples of the most frequent types of *"roles"* youngsters will assume in classroom life: leader, second in command, organizer, janitorial assistant, teacher's pet, model boy, black sheep, scapegoat, bully, isolate, rejectee, group executioner, attorney at law, defender of the innocent, group clown—with or against the adult—hero in battle, fifth columnist as to group interests, seducer and ringleader, trouble starter, rabblerouser, appeaser, humorous rescuer of tense situations, etc.

It is important to know these things about group roles: Which of such roles are well filled in your group? Which do not seem to have developed? Are the children who fill these roles doing so voluntarily (the boy who always provokes others into teasing him and then complains), or are they put there by group pressure (the undeserved outcast)? By what techniques did a youngster assume, keep, or lose his group role? How harmless, valuable, or disturbing to you personally, are certain group roles in your classroom life? [1]

[1] *Know Your Group*—mimeographed, 1943.

When the leader recognizes these different roles and which individuals tend to assume them (not only among children, but also among adolescents and adults), he knows what to expect in the group and what he can count upon as resources for showing his leadership in different situations. Indeed, the leader who knows his group in this way is like the orchestra conductor who knows all the different players and what they can and will do. Then, too, the leader who knows his group members and recognizes their customary roles can plan ahead in terms of what the group can do to help each member grow, mature, and, when desirable, change his role, as we shall explain later.

Few groups get organized or continue to meet without running into conflicts of beliefs, of ideas, of feelings. Controversy is especially frequent today because so many of our long-accepted ideas are being challenged. Also, groups today are increasingly composed of persons with widely different backgrounds and traditions.

It is hard, therefore, to discuss any topic or to plan any action without some difference of opinion, sometimes sharp conflicts. These disputes can wreck the group, or they can strengthen the group if they are handled constructively.

How to conduct a group while it resolves these conflicts is often a very difficult task which may test the leader's capacity strongly. There are some clues to these situations which every leader should know and utilize as essential aspects of his leadership.

But first it must be recognized that we cannot assume that everyone is rational and capable of listening and learning from discussion. Unfortunately, there are some persons who, though they are not "crazy" or "insane," are very rigid personalities and cannot tolerate anyone who differs from their ideas, especially in certain areas or topics. Moreover, there are some individuals with very strong beliefs and emotionally toned convictions which they want to express repeatedly. There are also some personalities who have developed chronic feelings of anxiety and who must have certainty at all costs. They are upset if they hear anyone voicing different opinions. Then, too, there are some personalities who are chronically hostile, feeling strong resentment toward the world and expressing their hostility to people without any justification. These persons react against anyone because they are "spoiling for a fight."

No group can prosper if it has too many of these unhappy personalities. Even one of them may be so disruptive that the group is continually disturbed and frustrated. When this occurs, the leader should consult someone about the wisdom of requesting these troublesome persons to leave the group, but this should not be done until the leader has made a genuine effort to create a harmonious group feeling. It is too easy to blame someone in the group for what may be the leader's failure to act as a constructive leader or to evoke leadership from the members. These troublemakers sometimes will respond positively when given an opportunity to exercise leadership or to carry some responsibility in the group.

Sometimes a leader has to deal with disorders in a group. One or two members may be inclined to roughhouse or to withdraw and talk together. Occasionally, there is one person who likes to create a distraction by trying to be "funny" and playing for a laugh on all occasions. If the leader tries to deal with these individuals by his own efforts—persuasion, commands, threats—he may lose his group and largely forfeit his leadership. Rather, the leader should talk over the situation with two or three members of the group whom he can rely upon as fairly stable and co-operative individuals. He can explain to them that the disturbing member is probably an unhappy person or a lonely person who does not know how to escape from these undesirable patterns. The question is, then, how the group can help him to give up these self-defeating activities and learn to contribute to the group. It has been found that when the group members, or at least some of them, realize that they can genuinely help, they are able to bring about astonishing improvement.

For example, when the group is aware that a disturbing member, who is continually clowning or trying to distract others' attention, needs group recognition, they can give that person a more active, responsible part in the group. This may transform him into a very productive member who finds in this new role a more satisfying and desirable pattern of conduct. Again, if the group is helped to recognize that the loud boastful member or one who talks all the time may be worried about his place or status in the group, they can be more friendly and appreciative of his contributions, showing him that he is accepted and valued. Thereby, he will discover that he does not have to boast or try to outtalk others in order to belong.

In almost every group, there is someone who is shy, passive, almost withdrawn, seldom speaking. Such individuals likewise can be encouraged to come out of their shells and to participate when they are shown that others like them and do not threaten them. This can be done by those individuals in the group who would other wise ignore such inactive individuals but who will take the trouble to be friendly and encouraging to these shy or timid persons. Learning to be helpful to the timid and retiring person provides opportunities for the strong and popular individual to develop his capacities for new relationships.

As the group members increasingly accept responsibility for helping one another by recognizing that undesirable or disturbing behavior or shy, passive behavior is usually a cry for help, they not only gain strength and increased confidence, but they also become aware of how much they owe to the leader who has enabled them to develop these capacities.

The leader functions as the one who suggests that the group, or initially a few members, should consider what might be done to help those needing group assistance of this kind. He may raise the questions: "How do you think X feels when he is clowning or talking too much or when he is sitting silent and not participating?" "What would you like the group to do or say, if you were X?" These questions may stimulate the group (or the subgroup) to try to realize what an individual may feel, how he regards the group and what may be going on in his "private world." The leader also can suggest ways in which to carry out or apply what they decide to try as ways of helping individuals. Thus the leader may appoint a committee or "working party" so that a member can be given the position of chairman or job leader with responsibility. To the committee he can also appoint members who will be likely to work well with the chairman, especially if they have been given some awareness of how they can function on that committee or "working party." In various ways the leader provides opportunities for each member of the group to modify or change his customary role and to learn new and more productive activities and relationships by sharing leadership with each member of the group. This sharing, however, must be done with care and discrimination. It is not enough to call upon members of the group in rotation to take the lead. The leader should increasingly recognize the points at which specific individuals are to be called upon to share leadership by making suggestions, undertaking tasks, stimulating discussion in situations where each can function most effectively. The leader should also provide opportunities for the less gifted, the less active or timid members to assume leadership when they can do so without too much tension or worry about their ability. Such shy, fearful individuals can be helped to gain confidence if they are given an opportunity to be successful in some situation—what is called "planned success."

By helping the group to handle the needs of individuals and these sometimes disturbing situations, the leader can strengthen his leadership and further the group process as the way to develop self-discipline and group loyalty.

There are many different kinds of personalities in almost every group, each with his own ideas and feelings, which he may assert vigorously and defend vehemently. Some may insist upon continually disagreeing with others, challenging every statement they make. Others may be ready to agree with any-one who speaks loudly and strongly.

Even the best-balanced individuals may have had little experience in groups except under an authoritarian leader. They have had little practice in discussion, as contrasted with arguments and disputes. They have no understanding of how individuals can contribute to a process of group thinking. Therefore it may take some time before the members of the group recognize the necessity for developing a more receptive attitude and welcoming participation by others. The leader is responsible for giving the members of a group some understanding of this kind of group thinking and for helping them to practice it.

First of all, it is necessary for the members of the group to be able and willing to listen to each other. Strange to say, that is one of the hardest things to learn. We ourselves are usually so eager to talk or to contradict what someone else is saying that we do not really listen or do not actually hear. And, if we do listen, we often fail to hear what the other person is saying—we hear what we expect to hear, and frequently that is not what the other person said.

In a group discussion, it is often worthwhile to ask each person who wants to speak against another's position to do this: he must first state in his own language what the other person actually said. Usually an attempt to do this shows that the speaker did not clearly hear or understand what the other person said, and so his remarks may be irrelevant and even misleading. It may take some time and patience to arrive at a satisfactory restatement of the point to be discussed, but this process may reduce much of the misunderstanding and confusion in the group.

The leader has a very important role in these discussions. He must be not only impartial but concerned with getting the issues clearly stated and understood before they are debated or fought over. This means the leader must keep the discussion from wandering all over or becoming "too hot."

One way of doing this is to remind the group that of course each one will see things in a different way. Hence, these differences need to be heard so that the group will be able to think clearly and recognize the various factors or aspects of the problem and to realize the full meaning of the subject they are discussing.

Another way of fostering discussion that may be productive is to divide the group into smaller units—"buzz sessions"—so that three or four can talk and try to clarify their ideas. Then each buzz session reports to the larger group. Sometimes it is wiser to appoint a "working party" to take time out of the group meeting to formulate a proposal for the whole group to discuss.

Parliamentary procedure is essential to many situations, but it is often an obstacle to good group practice. If no one can discuss anything until a specific proposal has been made as a motion and seconded, this means that discussion is usually limited to arguments for or against the proposed action or resolution. It is often more fruitful for the leader to state clearly what the problem is, or the need, and then ask each member of the group to say what he thinks is important or necessary for meeting that problem. In this way various aspects of a question can be examined, and all the available information can be heard *before* any specific proposal or motion is made or suggestion for action is formulated. This has the great advantage of letting everyone contribute to the thinking of the group instead of lining them up as for or against a motion.

Sometimes there are splits in a group—one part may want to do one thing, another part to do something different. Here the group itself must be encouraged to resolve this conflict. They can decide to hear one, then the other, or to seek an alternative plan in which all can join.

The leader in these situations of conflict or disagreement has the responsibility of keeping the issue or problem fluid, preventing premature closure or decision before the group has fully explored the question. Often in a group there are one or more members who are either impatient or eager to settle an issue in their own way. The leader can delay this hasty decision by seeing that everyone speaks and reminding the more expressive that they have been heard and now should listen to others.

8

leadership as personal development

It takes time to become an effective leader because leadership, as we have seen, has to be learned or developed as the leader grows and matures. When we are children or adolescents, we are usually chiefly concerned about ourselves, wrapped up in our own ideas and feeling and purposes. As we grow older and approach adulthood, we often become almost suddenly aware of others and usually we have some altruistic interests in improving the world, relieving the misery and suffering of people. We may dream of performing some great deeds, of redressing the wrongs in the world, and of making people happier. At the same time, we may be very critical of other people and the confusions and compromises they accept. We want to be better and to act more intelligently and helpfully for the world.

These altruistic feelings and aspirations are our most precious resources for human welfare; but they are often wasted because it is so hard to find any way of doing something concrete and effective. Sometimes, the most altruistic persons become discouraged and hide their disillusioned behavior behind a mask of cynicism and a hard-boiled attitude. This is a critical period in our development when we have to hold on to our altruism and our aspirations but realize that we must live and work with people if anything worth while is to be achieved.

Thus, we have to accept the often difficult task of growing up as a person, revising our earlier beliefs and expectations as we seek ways of living and working and establishing relationships with others on an adult level. This is a lifelong task because we must repeatedly revise our ideas and alter our conduct and relationships as we grow older and enter into new situations and accept new responsibilities.

Perhaps the most important lesson we learn is that we gain strength by generosity, by giving others of our interest, our time, our understanding; by helping others, we ourselves become stronger, more competent, and more capable of giving. For example, when we marry, we have an opportunity to cease being a self-centered person and begin to think and plan how to cherish, protect, and love another. When we become a parent and begin to care for a child, again we find that accepting this responsibility helps us to grow up, to become in our turn an adult who can be generous to the young. We also find that we must increasingly take into account what our wife or husband thinks and feels, if we are to develop a harmonious and mutually fulfilling relationship. This calls for increased awareness of others, deeper understanding of others, more empathy (the ability to feel with others) and also for more self-awareness and insight into our own personality.

As we face the tasks of living, meet the responsibilities of marriage, parenthood, family living and participation in our community, we gradually mature and unless we are too rigid, too inflexible, we relearn and revise our earlier patterns and relationships.

Some individuals do not mature in this way; and so they continue to be demanding children or persistent adolescents, unable to give up their earlier patterns and learn the new patterns and relationships that are appropriate, if not necessary, to their advancing years.

All this is relevant to the task of becoming an effective leader because the leader, as we have seen, must learn to be generous to others, capable of understanding and accepting those who are different from himself but who need his helpful guidance to grow up and mature. As in growing up, the leader must learn his roles and develop his skills. He will inevitably make mistakes, often fail to understand what is happening, or not realize until too late that he should have spoken or acted in a situation. However, this is more or less unavoidable, perhaps necessary, since we have to fumble and learn from our mistakes in many areas of human living. The crucial question is, Do we learn from our mistakes, do we reflect upon what we do and say and try to gain understanding for the next situation?

Being a leader is not an easy job. To lead in any kind of organization takes energy and strength and, above all, faith in people. To be able to function effectively, the leader must feel that he is trusted. When there is tension or conflict, the leader must never forget that these difficult times may be the most effective way to develop the loyalty and strength of his group, if he can help them to meet these problems constructively.

As he sees the group members learning to relate themselves to each other and to create an organized group which is responsive to him as he is responsive to them, the leader begins to find his own reward. But in addition, the leader needs to remember that what he is doing as a leader has a larger meaning than just his group program. He is helping his group to learn what self-government means and what the democratic ideal involves. He is helping his group members to discover how they can maintain a free society by learning to respect each other and to work together for their common goals. ₍

Citizenship is more than voting once a year, obeying the law and participating in representative government; it is an all-year-round, day-by-day activity, striving with others for the goal values we cherish and translating these into a way of life that genuinely respects the worth of each individual and recognizes human dignity in everyone. The leader who helps his group through experiences which foster their individual development and their capacity for group living, learning, working with others is helping to maintain a free country against the pressures and propaganda that today threaten the individual and tend to rob him of his dignity and personal significance. Also, he is helping his group to recognize that they can and must learn to work together to achieve any worthwhile objectives while continuing to be unique individuals.

This, as we all realize, is the democratic aspiration: to advance toward a society which becomes ever more social so that it can foster more genuine individuality of each person who, in turn, will help to evoke and maintain an ever-better social life. This may sound like a paradox, but only because we forget that we can be human personalities only in so far as we can relate ourselves to other personalities and increasingly attain some of the potentialities of our human nature in our varied human relations.

This gives the major clue to what modern leadership means, as no longer the expression of an aloof, domineering person, but rather as a shared, dynamic relationship in which, as we have seen, leadership operates by evoking from the group a circular, reciprocal, and creative process. Thus, leadership emerges as the way groups of persons today seek their common purposes, not *for* or *under* their leader, but *with* their leader.